Excel XLOOKUP and Other Lookup Functions

Create Easier and More Versatile Lookup Formulas with New Powerful Excel Functions

NATHAN GEORGE

CONTENTS

INTRODUCTION

XLOOKUP is a new and exciting function in Excel that supersedes VLOOKUP, HLOOKUP and even INDEX/MATCH. If you are new to Excel lookup functions or already familiar with previous lookup functions, you will learn easier and faster methods of creating lookup formulas.

In this book, we get to cover Excel lookup formulas in more depth, with more examples than would have been practical in a general-purpose Excel book. This book will walk you through multiple examples of how you can use XLOOKUP to create solutions for different scenarios in Excel, including specific examples to highlight some of XLOOKUP's differences and advantages over VLOOKUP.

Excel XLOOKUP and Other Lookup Functions also covers the new XMATCH function (which is a replacement for the old MATCH function) and how you can use INDEX/XMATCH/XMATCH to perform simultaneous vertical and horizontal lookups.

The FILTER and SORT functions are also new dynamic array functions that you can use to return multiple values based on your specified criteria.

The new dynamic array functions like XLOOKUP and FILTER are only available to Microsoft 365 subscribers (formerly Office 365). Thus, if you are using a perpetual license version of Office 2019 or Office 2016, XLOOKUP will not be available to you. For that reason, this book also covers the good old VLOOKUP in some depth. VLOOKUP is still an immensely popular and widely used function in Excel.

After reading this book, you will know how to use the new XLOOKUP function to create solutions for a variety of lookup tasks in Excel. You will also learn how to use the combination of INDEX/XMATCH/XMATCH to perform complex lookups, and how to use the FILTER and SORT functions to fetch and transform data.

Who Is This Book For?

This book is for you if you want to learn more about the new XLOOKUP and XMATCH functions in Excel. We also cover the VLOOKUP function in case you still need it. This book is not an introductory Excel book and requires some basic knowledge of Excel. You need to be familiar with creating formulas with functions in Excel.

If you need to brush up on the basics (or if you are new to Excel), then my *Excel 2019 Basics* book covers all the foundation knowledge you will need. I have created the lessons in this book using Excel 2019 in the Microsoft 365 suit.

Assumptions

The software assumptions made when writing this book is that you already have Excel installed on your computer and you are working on the Microsoft Windows platform (7, 8 or 10). If you are using Excel on a Mac, then substitute any Windows keyboard commands mentioned in the book for the Mac equivalent. All the features within Excel remain the same for both platforms.

If you are using Excel on a tablet or touchscreen device, again substitute any keyboard commands mentioned in the book with the equivalent on your touchscreen device.

Important: If you are using Microsoft 365 and you do not have XLOOKUP or XMATCH in your Excel installation, don't panic, it is on its way! Your Microsoft 365 installation may be on a semi-annual update plan, in which case you will get the update starting July 2020.

Practice Files

Included with this book are downloadable Excel files for all examples covered. This will enable you to follow the examples in this book, hands-on, without needing to create the sample data from scratch. You can practice by changing the data to view different results.

You can download the files from the following link:

https://www.excelbytes.com/xlookup-download

Note: The practice files are Excel 2019 files. You would need to have Excel installed on your computer to open and use these files (preferably Excel 2013 and above). Windows 10 comes with the functionality to unzip files, but if your OS does not have this feature, you will need to get a piece of software like WinZip or WinRAR to unzip the file.

1. HOW TO ENTER A FORMULA

There are several ways you can enter a formula in Excel. In this chapter, we will cover how to enter a formula directly in the formula bar and also how to use the Insert Function dialog box to find and enter functions.

To insert a formula/function in the formula bar, do the following:

1. Click in the cell where you want to display the result.

2. Click in the formula bar.

3. Enter your formula, starting your entry with the equal sign (=). This specifies that your entry is a formula and not a static value.

For example:

=SUM(A2:A10)

Function Library

| A11 | ▼ | ⋮ | ✕ | ✓ | f_x | =SUM(A2:A10)| |

⊿	A	B	C	D	E	F
1						
2	12					
3	40					
4	68					
5	96					
6	124					
7	152					
8	180					
9	208					
10	236					
11	A10)					
12						
13						

Tip: As much as possible, avoid typing cell references directly into the formula bar as it could introduce errors. To enter a function, type in the equal sign followed by the function, and then an open bracket. For example, enter **=SUM(**. Then using your mouse pointer, select the cells you want for the arguments in the worksheet itself before typing in the closing bracket.

The Insert Function Dialog Box

A second way you can enter a function is by using the **Insert Function** dialog box:

1. Select the cell where you want to insert the formula.

2. Click in the formula bar to place the cursor there and click the **Insert Function** button to the left of the formula bar (or the **Insert Function** command button on the **Formulas** tab on the Ribbon).

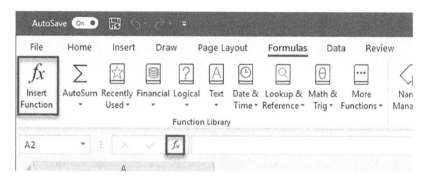

This will display the **Insert Function** dialog box. This dialog box provides the option to search for the function or select it from a category.

3. To search for the function, enter the name of the function in the **Search for a function** box. For example, if you are searching for the XLOOKUP function, you would enter XLOOKUP in the search box, select it from the list below, and click the **Go** button.

The **Select a function** list will display all the functions related to your search term.

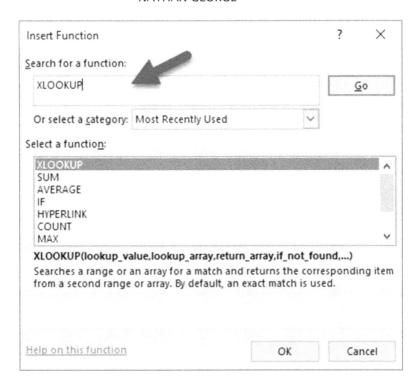

Note: If you do not have the XLOOKUP function yet, it will not show up on the list.

You can also use the **category** drop-down list to select a function if you know its category in Excel. For example, you can find the XLOOKUP function in the **Logical** category (if you have it). If you have used a function recently, it will be listed in the **Most Recently Used** category.

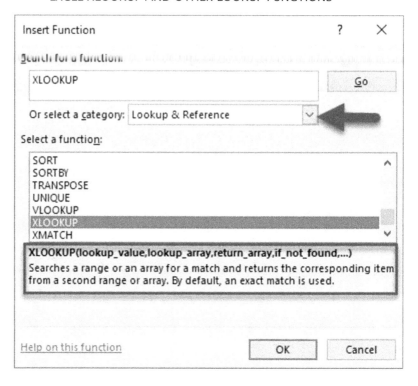

4. Select the function you want on the list. Below the list, you will see the syntax for the function and a description of what the function does.

5. Click **OK** to open the **Function Arguments** dialog box.

   The Function Arguments dialog box enables you to enter the arguments for the function. A function argument is a piece of data that the function needs to run.

   This dialog box is particularly useful if you are not familiar with a function as it describes each argument, shows a preview of the values in the arguments, and even the return value (if you click OK and use the Insert Function button to reopen the dialog box).

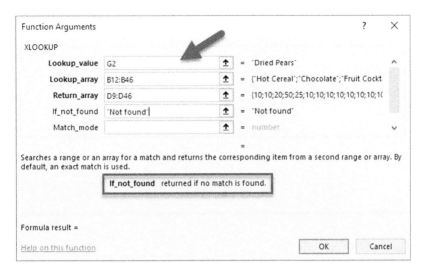

6. To enter a range for an argument, click the text box for the argument and select the range on your worksheet using your mouse pointer. Excel will automatically enter the range in the text box.

7. When done, click **OK** to insert the formula in your worksheet.

2. XLOOKUP FUNCTION

XLOOKUP is a new function introduced in 2020 in Excel as a replacement for the VLOOKUP function. Just like its predecessor, XLOOKUP searches a range or an array and returns a value corresponding to the first match it finds on the same row in another range. For instance, you can look up the *Price* of a product in a data list using the *product ID* or *Name*. Similarly, you can return the name of an employee using their employee ID. If XLOOKUP does not find a match, you can tell it to return the closest (approximate) match.

Unlike VLOOKUP, which only allows you to return values from a column to the right of the lookup range, XLOOKUP can return values from columns to the left or the right of the lookup range. XLOOKUP also returns exact matches by default, which makes it easier and more convenient to use than its predecessor.

Note: The XLOOKUP function is only available to Microsoft 365 users. If you are using a *one-time purchase* version of Excel 2019 or Excel 2016, XLOOKUP will not be available. If you are a Microsoft 365 subscriber and you cannot find this function, your Microsoft 365 installation may be on a semi-annual update plan, in which case you will get the update starting July 2020.

Key Features and Differences With VLOOKUP

One of the features that make XLOOKUP more flexible than VLOOKUP is that it uses separate lookup and return ranges, whereas VLOOKUP uses a single table array and then defines a column index number for the return column. Below are some key advantages XLOOKUP has over VLOOKUP.

- **Returns values from both sides of the lookup range**

  With VLOOKUP, you must have the column you are searching to the left of the column with the return value. XLOOKUP enables you to return values from anywhere in your worksheet, left, right, top or bottom. This means you no longer need to worry about rearranging your columns to perform a lookup.

- **Finds exact match by default**

  XLOOKUP looks for an exact match by default which ensures that new users will not accidentally return erroneous data. With VLOOKUP, if you want an exact match, you will have to specify that with an argument.

- **Insert or delete columns without disrupting the formula**

  With XLOOKUP, you can insert or delete columns in the lookup range and return range without the formula breaking. VLOOKUP uses a static numerical reference to specify the return range, so the formula breaks if you insert or delete columns in the table array without updating the formula.

- **Reverse lookup**

  XLOOKUP enables you to search your data list from both directions. From top to bottom or bottom to top. Hence you can find and return the last occurrence of a value in your list.

- **Returns a cell reference**

  A neat feature of XLOOKUP is that it can return a cell reference or range when nested. Hence, you can use it to create a range dynamically based on lookup values in your spreadsheet.

- **Array function**

  XLOOKUP can return a single value or a series of values that will "spill" into other cells. This is a feature previously only found in array functions. With recent Microsoft 365 updates, dynamic array formulas that can return multiple values will automatically spill them either down the column or across the row into neighbouring cells. This is called the **spill range**.

  Previously, array functions required you to first select the range for the output and then use Ctrl+Shift+Enter (CSE) to insert the result in the range. The spill range makes it a lot easier to use dynamic array formulas as you do not have to figure out how many cells you need to select for the result.

- **Built-in #N/A error handling**

  XLOOKUP enables you to specify a default value to return in place of an #N/A error if Excel cannot find the lookup value. To catch and handle #N/A errors when using VLOOKUP, you would need to nest your formula in the IFERROR function or IFNA function.

Syntax and Arguments

Syntax:

```
=XLOOKUP(lookup_value, lookup_array, return_array,
        [if_not_found], [match_mode],
        [search_mode])
```

Arguments and descriptions

Argument	Description
lookup_value	Required. What value are you searching for? Excel will look for a match for this value in the *lookup_array*. You can provide a value here or a cell reference containing the value you want to find.
lookup_array	Required. Where do you want to search? This is the lookup range containing the columns you want to include in your search, for example, A2:D10.
return_array	Required. Which range contains the values you want to return? This is the return range. The return range can have one or more columns as XLOOKUP is about to return more than one value.
[if_not_found]	Optional. This optional argument enables you to enter a piece of text to return if a valid match is not found. If this argument is omitted and a valid match is not found, #N/A will be returned.
[match_mode]	Optional. This optional argument enables you to specify a match mode from four options:

	0 (or omitted) = Exact match. If no match is found an error will be returned (#N/A). This is the default if you omit this argument.
	-1 - Exact match or the next smallest item, if an exact match is not found.
	1 - Exact match or the next largest item, if an exact match is not found.
	2 - Performs a wildcard match where you use *, ?, and ~. See the example below on using wildcards for more details on wildcard searches.
[search_mode]	Optional. This optional argument enables you to specify the order in which you want to perform the search:
	1 (or omitted) - Search first to last. This is the default if this argument is omitted.
	-1 - Perform the search in reverse order - last to first.
	2 - Perform a binary search for data sorted in ascending order. If lookup_array is not sorted in ascending order, invalid results will be returned.
	-2 - Perform a binary search for data sorted in descending order. If lookup_array is not sorted in descending order, invalid results will be returned.

Tip: Regarding the *search_mode* argument, in earlier versions of Excel, performing binary searches on sorted lists produced quicker results, but in Microsoft 365, non-binary searches are equally fast. Hence, it is no longer beneficial to use binary search options for sorted lists. It is easier to use 1 or -1 for the *search_mode* argument as it means you don't require a sorted table.

XLOOKUP Examples

The XLOOKUP function is very versatile and will enable the average Excel user to perform many tasks that previously would require multiple nested functions. Below are some examples demonstrating XLOOKUP.

Vertical Lookup

In this example, we are using XLOOKUP to return the reorder level of the product entered in cell F1. The formula is in cell F2.

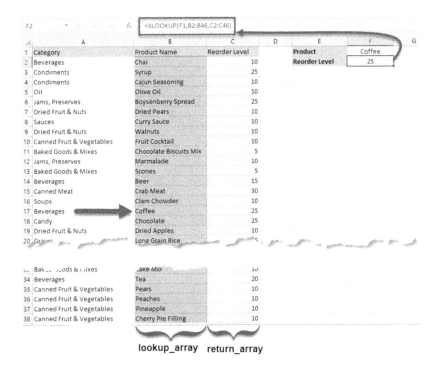

lookup_array   return_array

Formula explanation:

=XLOOKUP(F1,B2:B46,C2:C46)

The formula says, in range B2:B46, find the value in cell F1 (which in this case is "Coffee") and return the value on the same row in range C2:C46.

The *if_not_found* argument has not been provided here so if a match is not found it will return an error which is the default behaviour.

The VLOOKUP equivalent of this formula would look like this:

=VLOOKUP(F1,B2:C46,2,0)

One benefit of using the XLOOKUP equivalent over this formula is that if we decide at some point to insert a column between columns B and C, it will not break the formula.

The lookup_array does not need to be sorted because XLOOKUP will return an exact match by default.

Horizontal Lookup

XLOOKUP can perform both vertical and horizontal lookups. So, you can also use it in place of the HLOOKUP function.

In the example below, we can retrieve the value associated with a month using the name of the month.

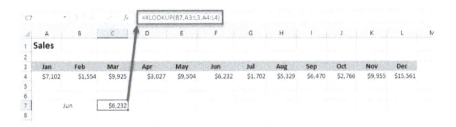

=XLOOKUP(B7,A3:L3,A4:L4)

The formula uses only the first 3 arguments of the XLOOKUP function. B7 is the lookup_value, A3:L3 is the lookup_array, and A4:L4 is the return_array.

Note that a horizontal lookup_array must contain the same number of columns as the return_array.

Simultaneous Vertical and Horizontal Lookup

In this example, we will use two XLOOKUP functions to perform both a vertical and horizontal match. Here, our formula will first look for a "Mark" in range A4:A15, then look for "Q3" in the top row of the table (range B3:E3) and return the value at the intersection of the two. Previously, you would need to use the INDEX/MATCH/MATCH combination to achieve the same result.

I4			f_x	=XLOOKUP(G4,A4:A15,XLOOKUP(H4,B3:E3,B4:E15))						
	A	B	C	D	E	F	G	H	I	J
1	Sales data									
2										
3	Salesperson	Q1	Q2	Q3	Q4					
4	Penny	17,526	23,972	61,066	22,596		Mark	Q3	19,062	
5	Leslie	49,405	36,646	21,899	62,629					
6	Sally	78,658	16,529	14,976	68,184					
7	Shaun	80,176	84,918	66,561	65,326					
8	Julie	86,988	29,692	30,197	80,960					
9	Velma	94,514	13,333	78,000	59,718					
10	Ian	23,183	21,547	40,408	57,767					
11	Cassandra	70,597	19,615	54,664	68,175					
12	Mark	16,832	91,907	19,062	22,167					
13	Kathy	45,446	14,638	52,312	92,069					
14	Renee	34,583	78,213	21,295	26,964					
15	Judith	18,689	91,081	66,795	96,860					

Formula explanation:

=XLOOKUP(G4,A4:A15,XLOOKUP(H4,B3:E3,B4:E15))

The first XLOOKUP function has the following arguments:
- lookup_value = G4
- lookup_array = A4:A15
- return_array = XLOOKUP(H4,B3:E3,B4:E15)

The second XLOOKUP, which is executed first, performs a horizontal search on B3:E3, using the value in cell H4 (which is "Q3") as the lookup_value, then returns the range **D4:D15**. Notice that the second XLOOKUP returns a range rather than a value. This range is what is used as the return_array argument for the first XLOOKUP.

So, after the second XLOOKUP has been executed, the first XLOOKUP will look like this:

=XLOOKUP(G4,A4:A15,D4:D15)

To examine how the formula performs the task, you can use the **Evaluate Formula** dialog box in Excel to see how each part of the formula is evaluated.

Follow the steps below to open the Evaluate Formula dialog box:

1. Select the cell with the formula you want to evaluate. In this case, it is cell **I4**.

2. On the Formulas tab, in the **Formula Auditing** group, click the **Evaluate Formula** command button.

3. In the Evaluate Formula dialog box, continue clicking the **Evaluate** button until the second XLOOKUP function has been evaluated and its result displayed as an argument to the first XLOOKUP function. For our example, you will need to click the Evaluate button three times.

You will notice that the second XLOOKUP performs a search using the lookup_value, "Q3", and then returns the range **D4:D15** (displayed as an absolute reference $D$4:D15). We can use XLOOKUP here as the *return_array* argument of the first XLOOKUP function because XLOOKUP can return a range as well as a value.

Next, the main XLOOKUP then performs a lookup using the value in cell G4, "Mark" as the lookup_value, cells A4:A15 as the lookup_array, and cells D4:D15 as the return_array to return the final result.

Return Multiple Values with Horizontal Spill

In this example, we want to be able to enter the name of a sales rep and return the number of orders and sales associated with them. This means the function will return more than one value. XLOOKUP is also an array function in that it can return an array of values from the return_array.

In the formula below, the lookup_value is in cell G2, the lookup_array argument is range A2:A12 and the return_array argument is range C2:D12.

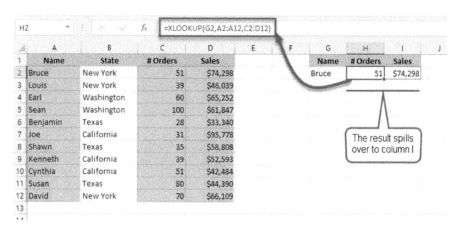

Formula explanation:

=XLOOKUP(G2,A2:A12,C2:D12)

As you can see from the formula, the return_array contains columns C and D. So, when we enter the name "Bruce" in cell G2, XLOOKUP returns the values in columns C and D from the same row. As the function returns more than one value, the result spills into cell I2.

The range containing the spilled result has a blue border around it. This is how you can tell that the result has spilled into other cells.

Return Multiple Values with Vertical Spill

To get the formula to spill vertically, we can use another example where we need to return the sales for more than one person on our list.

In this example, we first use the FILTER function to generate a filtered list of *Names* based in the *State* "New York". The function returns an array of names that spill vertically in the range G2:G4.

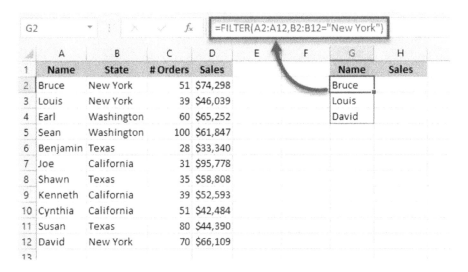

Note: FILTER is a relatively new dynamic array function in Excel that will become fully available to all Microsoft 365 users from July 2020 (if you do not already have it). For more on FILTER, see Chapter 5 in this book.

Next, we want to get the *Sales* associated to the names on our filtered list and insert them in column H. To do this, we use XLOOKUP in cell H2 and select cells G2:G4 for our lookup_value argument.

When you select your lookup_value on the worksheet (G2:G4), XLOOKUP will recognise the range as the return value of a dynamic array and will indicate that in the formula with a hash (#).

| H2 | | | | f_x | =XLOOKUP(G2#,A2:A12,D2:D12) |

	A	B	C	D	E	F	G	H	I
1	Name	State	# Orders	Sales			Name	Sales	
2	Bruce	New York	51	$74,298			Bruce	$74,298	
3	Louis	New York	39	$46,039			Louis	$46,039	
4	Earl	Washington	60	$65,252			David	$66,109	
5	Sean	Washington	100	$61,847					
6	Benjamin	Texas	28	$33,340					
7	Joe	California	31	$95,778					
8	Shawn	Texas	35	$58,808					
9	Kenneth	California	39	$52,593					
10	Cynthia	California	51	$42,484					
11	Susan	Texas	80	$44,390					
12	David	New York	70	$66,109					

Formula explanation:

=XLOOKUP(G2#,A2:A12,D2:D12)

The lookup_value argument in the formula is **G2#**.

G2# (note the hash) designates the entire range of the spill data. It tells us that G2 is the starting point of the array of values returned from a dynamic array formula.

The lookup_array is the Name column (A2:A12), and the return_array is the Sales column (D2:D12).

When you type in the formula in cell H2 and press Enter, XLOOKUP will return all the sales associated to the names in the dynamic array in column G. As we have more than one value, it will spill down vertically in column H2.

One benefit of using XLOOKUP like this is that the formula will dynamically adjust to the dynamic array in column G. For example, if the filter is changed and there are more names on the list, the formula in cell H2 will still work in returning the corresponding sales values. We don't have to worry about copying the formula down to additional cells.

Return Multiple Values from Non-Contiguous Ranges

Normally, to specify a return array for XLOOKUP, you have to select a range with contiguous columns. But what if we wanted to use non-contiguous columns for our return_array argument?

This is where the CHOOSE function comes to the rescue. You can use CHOOSE to select and return values or cell references from different columns in your worksheet, whether contiguous or non-contiguous.

So, if we use CHOOSE for our return_array in XLOOKUP, the formula will look like this:

=XLOOKUP(G2,A2:A12,CHOOSE({1,2},D2:D12,B2:B12))

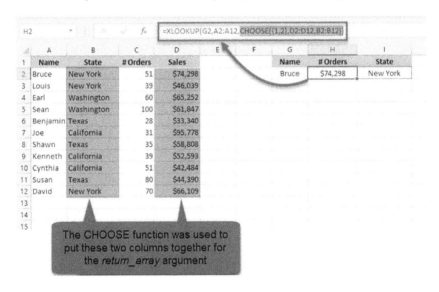

The CHOOSE function was used to put these two columns together for the *return_array* argument

This example is like Example 1 above, with the only difference being that we want to return the corresponding **Sales** and **State** for "Bruce". As the Sales and State are not in adjacent columns, we can use CHOOSE({1,2},D2:D12,B2:B12) to select and return the values in range D2:D12 and range B2:B12 as the return array for the XLOOKUP function.

Dynamic Range with **XLOOKUP**

In this example, we use XLOOKUP to return a dynamic range of values based on a set of criteria. In the past, you would need functions like OFFSET or INDEX and MATCH to create a dynamic range like this.

In the example below, we want to sum up the *Sales* of several records based on their order date. We can use the SUM function with two nested XLOOKUP functions to accomplish this task.

Note: The dates for this example are in the format: mm/dd/yyyy.

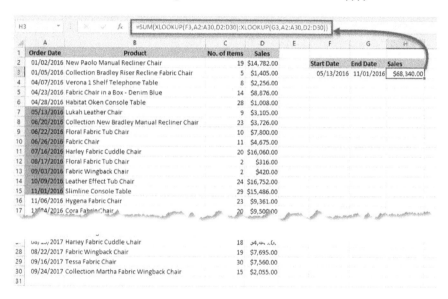

Formula explanation:

=SUM(XLOOKUP(F3,A2:A30,D2:D30):XLOOKUP(G3,A2:A30,D2:D30))

The formula uses two nested XLOOKUP functions to create a range dynamically by returning the starting cell and ending cell on either side of the colon range operator. The first XLOOKUP returns the first cell reference in the range, and the second XLOOKUP returns the last cell reference in the range.

After the nested functions have been executed, the SUM function would look like this:

=SUM(D7:D15)

You can use the **Evaluate Formula** dialog box to observe how the XLOOKUP functions are being evaluated and their return result.

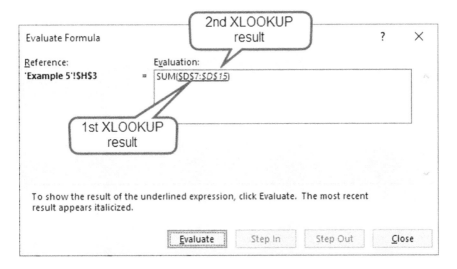

For more on how to evaluate a formula, see chapter 7.

You may wonder if we could have used the SUMIF function to perform the same task. SUMIF does not work for a scenario like this because we want to sum up a range of values using a starting criterion and an ending criterion for the range.

Handling #N/A Errors

With VLOOKUP, if a match is not found (and you have chosen FALSE for the range_lookup argument), you will get an #N/A error. Hence, you would need to combine VLOOKUP with the IFNA function (or IFERROR function) to catch #N/A errors and then return a custom value.

XLOOKUP improves on this by having a built-in feature to handle #N/A errors, so we no longer need other functions to catch those dreaded #N/A errors. XLOOKUP has a fourth argument, *if_not_found* that allows us to specify a value to be returned if a match is not found.

In the example below, we have entered the text 'Item not found' in the if_not_found argument. You can also enter a number, a cell reference, another formula, or an array.

=XLOOKUP(F2,B2:B12,D2:D12,"Item not found")

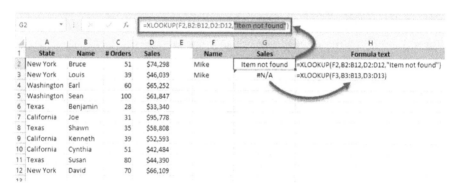

Note that if you omit the *if_not_found* argument and a match is not found, XLOOKUP will return #N/A.

Note: You will still need IFERROR for trapping errors other than #N/A. However, other errors may mean there is a problem with your formula that needs fixing rather than being trapped. For more on the IFERROR function, see chapter 6 in this book.

Find the Last Value First

By default, XLOOKUP searches from the first record in the list to the last record, and if you omit the *search_mode* argument, the default will be 1.

In the example below, we have used **-1** in the search_mode argument to tell XLOOKUP to search from the bottom up, hence finding the last matching value first. The last entry for "Texas" in the State column has a corresponding sale value of $44,390.

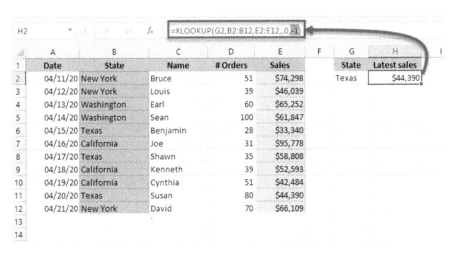

As you enter the formula, when your cursor is in the position of the final argument, you will get a drop-down list that allows you to select a value for the *search_mode* argument. When you click on a value on the list, you will see a tooltip (to its right) describing what that option does. To select a value on the list, highlight it using your up/down arrow keys and then press **Tab**.

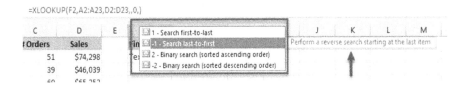

A note on binary searches

You will notice on the list of values for the search_mode argument that you can perform binary searches for sorted lists using 2 or -2. In earlier versions of Excel, performing binary searches on sorted lists produced quicker results, but with the latest version of Microsoft 365, non-binary searches are equally fast. Hence, there is no longer a benefit to using the binary search options on the list. It is easier to use 1 or -1 for the search_mode argument as they do not require the table to be sorted.

XLOOKUP Left

One limitation of VLOOKUP is that you can only return values in a column to the right of the lookup range. XLOOKUP solves this problem by enabling you to reference the lookup range and return ranges as separate arguments, hence these ranges can be anywhere in your worksheet, to the left or right of each other, and the formula will still work.

In the example below, let's say we have been tasked with adding the product code to the list of orders. The product codes can be found in the Product list to the right of the Orders.

To get the product code for each item on the list, we use XLOOKUP to find the product name on the product list and then return the corresponding product code on the same row.

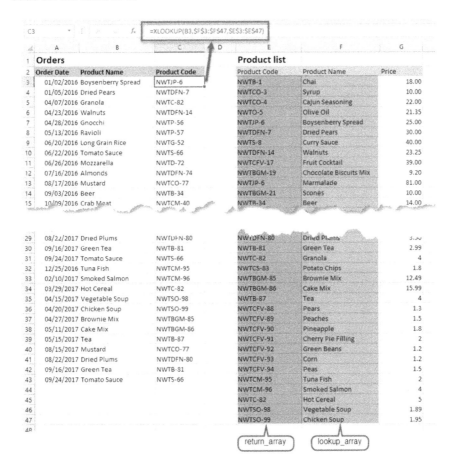

Formula explanation:

=XLOOKUP(B3,$F$3:$F$47,$E$3:$E$47)

The formula's lookup_value (the criteria being used for the search) is in cell B3.

The lookup_array and return_array arguments are F3:F47 and E3:E47. Note that return_array is to the left of lookup_array. This would not have been possible using VLOOKUP on its own.

The lookup range and return range have been set to absolute references ($F$3:$F$47,$E$3:$E$47). This enables us to fill down the formula in column D without the cell references changing for those two arrays.

Tip: To convert a cell reference to an absolute reference, select the reference in the formula bar and press the **F4** key. You can also type in the dollar signs manually, but it is faster (and less error-prone) to use F4. An absolute reference ensures the referenced cells do not change relatively when the formula is filled down to other cells.

Using Wildcards with **XLOOKUP**

XLOOKUP supports using wildcards for partial matches, but you need to add an asterisk before and after the search term. We have to set the *match_mode* argument to **2**, which tells the function to perform a wildcard match.

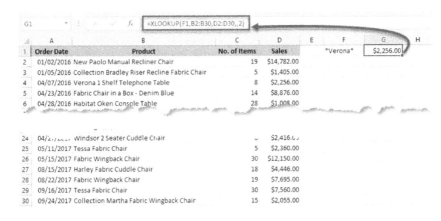

=XLOOKUP(F1,B2:B30,D2:D30,,2)

The lookup_value is the formula in cell F1, which has the partial search term *Verona*.

If you entered the search term directly in the formula, you would enclose it in quotes and the formula would look like this:

=XLOOKUP("*Verona*",B2:B30,D2:D30,,2)

Note that the *match_mode* argument is set to **2**, which specifies that we want a wildcard character match.

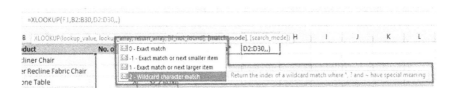

You can use the following wildcard characters to perform partial searches:

Use	To find
? (question mark)	Any single character. For example, "Wh?te" will find "White" and "Whyte".
* (asterisk)	Any number of characters. For example, *west finds "Northwest" and "Southwest".
~ (tilde) followed by ?, *, or ~	A question mark, asterisk, or tilde. When you place a tilde in front of a wildcard character, it will be treated as ordinary text. For example, B11~? finds "B11?".

Finding an Approximate Match

In the previous example, we used the match_mode argument to return a partial match using a wildcard character. We can also use the match_mode argument to return an approximate match by setting it to -1.

In the example below, we want to match a grade to each score on the list using our grade table.

C3			fx	=XLOOKUP(B3,$F$3:$F$6,$G$3:$G$6,,-1)		
	A	B	C	D E	F	G
1	Exam results				Grade table	
2	Student	Score	Grade		Score	Grade
3	Bruce	73	Merit		70	Merit
4	Louis	20	Fail		50	Credit
5	Earl	39	Pass		35	Pass
6	Sean	81	Merit		0	Fail
7	Benjamin	60	Credit			
8	Joe	19	Fail			
9	Shawn	51	Credit			
10	Kenneth	42	Pass			
11	Cynthia	79	Merit			
12	Susan	51	Credit			

Formula explanation:

=XLOOKUP(B3,$F$3:$F$6,$G$3:$G$6,,-1)

The formula has -1 as the match_mode argument, which finds an exact match or the next smaller item in the lookup_array (which is F3:F6 set to an absolute reference). The function then returns the corresponding grade in the return_array (G3:E6 F6).

Note that the lookup_array and return_array have been set to absolute references in the formula to enable us to fill it down to the other cells in column C without changing the cell references for those two arrays.

Tip: Instead of absolute references, you can use named ranges for the lookup_array and return_array when you intend to fill down the formula to multiple cells. A named ranged is an absolute reference by default, and in certain circumstances will make the formula easier to understand.

Common **XLOOKUP** Errors and Solutions

- **#N/A error**

  If an exact match is not found, and the *if_not_found* and *match_mode* arguments are omitted, then XLOOKUP will return an #N/A error.

  There may be scenarios where you will not know if your formula will generate this error, for example, when it is filled down to multiple cells in a column. If you want to replace the #N/A error with a meaningful message, then specify it in the if_not_found argument.

  For example:

  =XLOOKUP(F2,B2:B12,D2:D12,"Item not found")

- **#VALUE! error**

  This error is often generated because the lookup array and return array are not the same length. When you get this error, check that these ranges are the same length. If you are performing a vertical lookup, they should have the same number of rows. If you are carrying out a horizontal lookup, they should have the same number of columns.

- **#NAME? in cell**

  The #NAME? error value usually means that there is something wrong with the cell references. A typo in the cell reference or omitting the colon can generate this error. When you get this error, check your cell references. To help avoid errors and typos in cell references, select them on the worksheet with your mouse rather than typing them in the formula.

- **#REF! error**

  If XLOOKUP is referencing another workbook that is closed, you will get a #REF! error. To avoid this error, ensure all workbooks referenced in your formula are open.

- **#SPILL! Error**

  When returning multiple values, if there is already data in the spill range, a #SPILL! error will be returned. To avoid this error, ensure there is no data in the range that will contain the returned results.

3. VLOOKUP FUNCTION

With the introduction of XLOOKUP, the VLOOKUP function (and the less popular HLOOKUP) are now legacy functions in Excel. XLOOKUP should be your go-to function for any task for which you would have previously used VLOOKUP. XLOOKUP is easier to use, more intuitive, and richer in terms of functionality.

So why cover VLOOKUP here?

Here are a couple of reasons why VLOOKUP will still be relevant for some time:

- If you have a perpetual license version of Excel 2016 or Excel 2019, you will not have access to XLOOKUP. VLOOKUP will still be what you would use for lookups until the next version of Excel.

- If you intend to send your worksheet to someone with a perpetual license version of Excel, you may want to use VLOOKUP for any lookup tasks because formulas with XLOOKUP will not work when they open your worksheet.

- In an organization, you may encounter VLOOKUP in formulas while maintaining existing worksheets.

The VLOOKUP function (vertical lookup) is one of the most commonly used lookup functions in Excel. VLOOKUP is an updated version of the legacy LOOKUP function, which is still available in Excel (for backward compatibility).

VLOOKUP enables you to find one piece of information in a workbook based on another piece of information. For example, if you have a *Products* table, you can find and return the *Product Code* by providing the *Product Name* to the VLOOKUP function.

Syntax and Arguments

Syntax

```
= VLOOKUP (lookup_value, table_array,
          col_index_num, [range_lookup])
```

Arguments

Argument	Description
lookup_value	Required. What value are you searching for? This is the lookup value. Excel will look for a match for this value in the leftmost column of your chosen range. You can provide a value here or a cell reference.
table_array	Required. What columns do you want to search? This is the lookup table containing the columns you want to include in your search e.g. A2:D10.
col_index_num	Required. Which column contains the search result? In table_array, starting from 1, count from the first column to determine what this number should be.
range_lookup	Optional. If you want an exact match, enter FALSE or 0 here. However, if an approximate match is OK, then enter TRUE or 1. For TRUE, you would need to sort the leftmost column in ascending order for correct results. This is an optional argument and if omitted the default will be TRUE.

Standard **VLOOKUP** Example

In the example below, we use VLOOKUP to find the *Price* and *Reorder Level* of a product by entering the product name in cell G2. The formula is in cell G3, and as you can see from the image below, it searches the table for *Dried Pears* and returns the price from the second column in our table array (B2:D46).

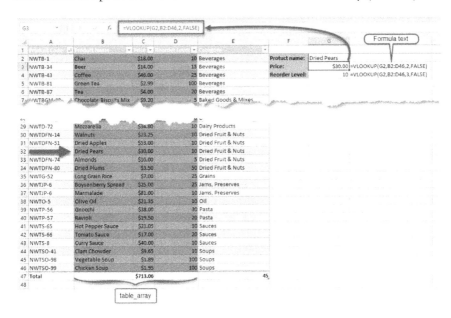

Formula Explanation:

To look up the **Price** for "Dried Pears" the formula is:

=VLOOKUP(G2, B2:D46, 2, FALSE)

The formula uses a lookup value in cell G2 to search a table array which is B2:D46.

The col_index_num argument is **2**, meaning we want VLOOKUP to search the first column, and once a match is found, return the value on the same row in the second column of table_array, which is the **Price** column.

The range_lookup is **FALSE**, which tells VLOOKUP that we want an exact match.

To look up the **Reorder Level** for Dried Pears we use the same formula and just change the col_index_num argument to 3, meaning we want to return values from the third column in table_array, which is the Reorder Level column.

=VLOOKUP(G2, B2:D46, **3**, FALSE)

Here, the VLOOKUP search for Dried Pears returns a Reorder Level of **10**.

Finding an Approximate Match with VLOOKUP

In the following example, we want to calculate the commission each Sales Rep is entitled to, based on their sales. We have a Commission table to the right of the Sales report with a graduated scale of rates against sales.

We want to ensure that if an exact match is not found on the commission table that an approximate match is applied for the sales rep. $5,000 or more in sales is 2% commission, $10,000 or more is 5%, $20,000 or more is 10%, and so on.

C3				f_x	=VLOOKUP(B3,table_array,2,TRUE)	
	A	B	C	D	E	F
1	**Sales**				**Commission table**	
2	**Sales Rep**	**Sales**	**Commisson**		**Sales**	**Rate**
3	Berna Alger	$7,372	2%		$0	0%
4	Rich Donaldson	$23,895	10%		$5,000	2%
5	Erwin Wofford	$31,323	15%		$10,000	5%
6	Arvilla Leon	$3,024	0%		$20,000	10%
7	Simone Sharkey	$73,033	25%		$30,000	15%
8	Guillermina Canales	$7,735	2%		$40,000	20%
9	Stacey Lovett	$22,417	10%		$50,000	25%
10	Jaunita Headrick	$1,483	0%			
11	Romaine Ashford	$9,028	2%			
12	Juliann Keane	$26,980	10%			
13						

Formula Explanation:

=VLOOKUP(B3,table_array,2,TRUE)

The *lookup_value* is cell B3 which is the value for which we want an approximate match in the lookup range (cells E3:F9).

Note that the lookup range (E3:F9) is named **table_array**. This is known as a named range. The benefit of using named ranges in formulas you want to fill down is that a named range is an absolute reference. This ensures the cell references you want to remain the same will not change as you fill down the formula.

The *col_index_num* is set to 2. This means we want to return values from the second column in table_array.

The optional *range_lookup* argument is set to TRUE which tells Excel to return an approximate match if an exact match is not found. The default for the *range_lookup* argument is TRUE if omitted so you do not need to set this argument explicitly to TRUE. I have entered it here for demonstration purposes only.

Using VLOOKUP and the CHOOSE Function for Left Lookups

In this example, we want to add the product code to the list of orders on the left of the worksheet below. The product codes can be found in the *Product list* to the right of the *Orders*.

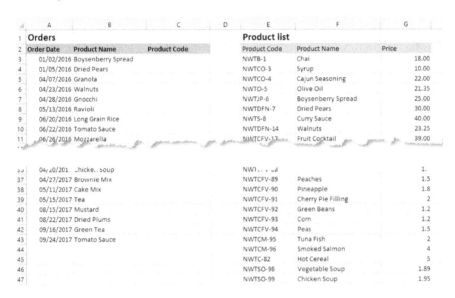

One limitation of VLOOKUP is that we can only return values in a column to the right of the lookup range. Our lookup range, in this case, is F3:F47 and the return range is E3:E47. The return values are in a column to the left of the lookup column.

To solve this problem, we can use the CHOOSE function to rearrange the columns for the table_array argument of VLOOKUP.

A Quick Look at the CHOOSE Function

Before progressing to the example, we need to first look at what the CHOOSE function does. My Excel 2019 Functions book covers the CHOOSE function in detail, but for our purposes here, we need to briefly look at the syntax and arguments.

Syntax

=CHOOSE(index_num, value1, [value2], ...)

Arguments

- **index_num**

  Required. This represents the value(s) you want to select from the list of arguments. This can be a number between 1 and 254, a formula, a cell that has a number between 1 and 254.

- **value1**

  Required. The first value is required. Values can be numbers, cell references, ranges, formulas, functions, or text. For this example, we will be using ranges.

- **[value2], ...**

  Optional. You can add up to 253 additional values.

When we apply the CHOOSE function to our formula, we get the following:

=VLOOKUP(B3,CHOOSE({1,2},$F$3:$F$47,$E$3:$E$47),2,FALSE)

	C3				f_x	=VLOOKUP(B3,CHOOSE({1,2},$F$3:$F$47,$E$3:$E$47),2,FALSE)		
	A	B		C	D	E	F	G	H
1	**Orders**					**Product list**		
2	Order Date	Product Name		Product Code		Product Code	Product Name	Price
3	01/02/2016	Boysenberry Spread		NWTJP-6		NWTB-1	Chai	18.00
4	01/05/2016	Dried Pears		NWTDFN-7		NWTCO-3	Syrup	10.00
5	04/07/2016	Granola		NWTC-82		NWTCO-4	Cajun Seasoning	22.00
6	04/23/2016	Walnuts		NWTDFN-14		NWTO-5	Olive Oil	21.35
7	04/28/2016	Gnocchi		NWTP-56		NWTJP-6	Boysenberry Spread	25.00
8	05/13/2016	Ravioli		NWTP-57		NWTDFN-7	Dried Pears	30.00
9	06/20/2016	ng Grain Rice		NWTG-52		NWTS-8	v Sauce	0.00
36	2	17 Chicke		NWTSO-55		NWTCFV-	Pears	1.3
37	04/27/2017	Brownie Mix		NWTBGM-85		NWTCFV-89	Peaches	1.5
38	05/11/2017	Cake Mix		NWTBGM-86		NWTCFV-90	Pineapple	1.8
39	05/15/2017	Tea		NWTB-87		NWTCFV-91	Cherry Pie Filling	2
40	08/15/2017	Mustard		NWTCO-77		NWTCFV-92	Green Beans	1.2
41	08/22/2017	Dried Plums		NWTDFN-80		NWTCFV-93	Corn	1.2
42	09/16/2017	Green Tea		NWTB-81		NWTCFV-94	Peas	1.5
43	09/24/2017	Tomato Sauce		NWTS-66		NWTCM-95	Tuna Fish	2
44						NWTCM-96	Smoked Salmon	4
45						NWTC-82	Hot Cereal	5
46						NWTSO-98	Vegetable Soup	1.89
47						NWTSO-99	Chicken Soup	1.95
48								

CHOOSE column 2 · CHOOSE column 1

Formula explanation:

=VLOOKUP(B3,CHOOSE({1,2},$F$3:$F$47,$E$3:$E$47),2,FALSE)

Our table_array is E3:F47 and we want to return values in column E. We want a method in our formula that reverses the order of the columns, that is, put column E to the right of column F. The CHOOSE formula can do this:

CHOOSE({1,2},$F$3:$F$47,$E$3:$E$47)

This formula has F3:F47 as the *value1* argument and E3:E47 as the *value2* argument. Both ranges have been converted to absolute references.

The *index_num* argument of our CHOOSE function is {1,2}, which tells the function to return the data in the order *value1* and *value2*, that is, column F before column E.

With the range (E3:E47) as the second column in table_array, VLOOKUP can now lookup values in the first column (F3:F17), and return values from the second column E3:E47.

To populate the other cells in column C, we can fill down the formula. The absolute references we have used means the lookup and return ranges remain the same.

Tip: We can make this formula a little easier to understand by using full column references as long as there will be no other data in the columns apart from the data being used by the formula.

With full column references, the formula would look like this:

=VLOOKUP(B3,CHOOSE({1,2},F:F,E:E),2,FALSE)

VLOOKUP and Error Handling

When using the VLOOKUP formula in Excel, sometimes you may encounter the #N/A error, which happens when the formula cannot find the lookup value.

When handling errors caused by VLOOKUP, you want to make sure you are using the right formula for your scenario. In this example, we will cover how to use the IFERROR function or the IFNA function with VLOOKUP to show something meaningful in place of an error.

In the example below, we use both IFERROR and IFNA to trap the same error.

Note: For the syntax and arguments of IFERROR and IFNA, see chapter 6 in this book.

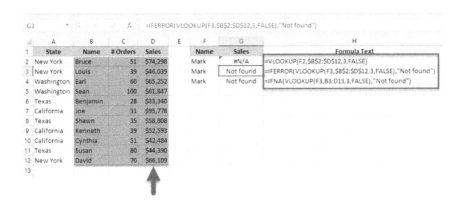

Formula explanation:

=VLOOKUP(F2,$B$2:$D$12,3,FALSE)

The formula is using the lookup value in cell F2 to search the table array (B2:D12) and return the *Sales* on the same row on column D. The lookup value we have used, "Mark", is not on the list of names in column B so the formula generates an #N/A error in cell G3.

=IFERROR(VLOOKUP(F3,$B$2:$D$12,3,FALSE),"Not found")

This formula is performing the same task as the first formula, but this time it is wrapped in an IFERROR function. IFERROR traps the #N/A error and returns "Not found" which is the value we have specified in the *value_if_error* argument.

=IFNA(VLOOKUP(F3,B3:D13,3,FALSE),"Not found")

The above VLOOKUP formula is nested in an IFNA function which traps the #N/A error and returns our specified value, "Not found".

VLOOKUP and Wildcards

VLOOKUP supports using wildcards for partial matches, but you need to use ampersands to concatenate an asterisk before and after the lookup_value argument.

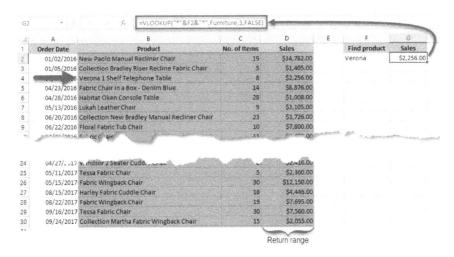

Return range

Formula explanation:

=VLOOKUP("*"&F2&"*",Furniture,3,FALSE)

Our lookup_value is "*"&F2&"*". The expression concatenates an asterisk to either side of the cell with the search term. So, the search term in this example will evaluate to *Verona*. This tells the formula to find the first item on the list with "Verona" anywhere within the string.

The table_array argument is a range named Furniture, which is range B2:D30. Our col_index_num (the return range) is 3. This is column D which is the third column in table_array.

A wildcard search requires you to set the range_lookup argument to FALSE, i.e. an exact match. This means if your search term is not found anywhere in your list, VLOOKUP will return an error.

Best Practices for VLOOKUP

- **Use absolute references for the table array.**

  Using absolute references allows you to fill-down a formula without having the cell references change. An absolute reference ensures VLOOKUP always looks at the same table array even when the formula is filled to other cells.

- **Do not store a number or date as a text value.**

  When searching for numbers or dates, ensure the data in the first column of the table array is not stored as text. Otherwise, the formula might return an incorrect or unexpected value. Number and date values are right-aligned while text values are left-aligned by default. Therefore, if your numbers or dates are left-aligned in the cell, you need to check that they are using the right cell format.

- **Sort the first column.**

  If you want VLOOKUP to find the next best match, that is, the range_lookup argument is TRUE, then make sure the first column in table_array is sorted.

- **Use wildcard characters.**

  You can use a wildcard in lookup_value if range_lookup is FALSE and lookup_value is text. A question mark (?) matches any single character, and an asterisk (*) matches any sequence of characters. If you want to find an actual question mark or asterisk as part of the text in table_array, type a tilde (~) in front of the character.

  For example, =VLOOKUP("Dried*",B2:D46,2,FALSE) will find the first item starting with "Dried" in the first column of table_array.

- **Make sure your data does not contain erroneous characters.**

  If you are searching for text values in the first column of the table array, ensure the data in the first column does not have leading or trailing spaces, non-printable characters, and inconsistent use of straight and curly quotation marks. In cases like these, the formula might return an unexpected value.

To clean up your data you can use the TRIM function to remove any extra spaces or the CLEAN function to removes all nonprintable characters.

Common Errors and Solutions

- **Wrong value returned**

  If you omit the range_lookup argument or set it to TRUE (that is, for an approximate match), you need to sort the first column of table_array alphabetically or numerically. If the first column is not sorted, the return value might be something unexpected. So, either use FALSE for an exact match or sort the first column of the table array if you want an approximate match.

- **#N/A error in cell**

  If the range_lookup argument is FALSE, and an exact match is not found you will get an #N/A error. You will also get an #N/A error if range_lookup is TRUE, and the lookup_value is smaller than the smallest value in the first column of table_array.

- **#REF! in cell**

  You will get the #REF error if the col_index_num argument is greater than the number of columns in the table array.

- **#VALUE! in cell**

  You will encounter a #VALUE! error if lookup_value argument is over 255 characters. Use wildcards for partial matches if the values in the lookup range are over 255 characters.

  The #VALUE! error will also be generated if the col_index_num argument contains text or is less than 1. Ensure col_index_num is not less than 1.

- **#NAME? in cell**

  The #NAME? error value usually means that the formula is missing quotes. If you enter a text value directly in your formula (instead of a cell reference) make sure you enclose the value in quotes. For example, =VLOOKUP("Dried Pears", B2:D46, 2, FALSE). You will also get this error if you make a mistake when typing in the cell reference. To avoid cell reference typos, select cell references on the worksheet with your mouse rather than typing them in the formula.

4. USING INDEX AND XMATCH FOR LOOKUPS

Another way you can carry out lookups in Excel is to use the combination of INDEX and MATCH. Traditionally, the INDEX/MATCH/MATCH combination was used for simultaneous vertical and horizontal matches. However, with the introduction of XLOOKUP, we can now perform simultaneous vertical and horizontal matches by using two XLOOKUP functions in a formula.

Naturally, XLOOKUP should do away with the INDEX/MATCH/MATCH combination. But not so fast! The introduction of the new XMATCH function makes the INDEX/XMATCH/XMATCH combination an interesting prospect, and some would argue, an easier way to perform simultaneous vertical and horizontal matches. This is why we will be looking at INDEX and XMATCH here.

Before we delve into using both functions together, we first need to go over each function individually, their syntax and description of arguments.

XMATCH Function

The XMATCH function is an improved version of the MATCH function. The MATCH function searches for a given item in a list and then returns the relative position of the item in the list. That means, MATCH tells you where in your list you can locate the value you have provided as the lookup value.

For example, if the range A1:A5 has the values 10, 30, 26, 44, and 100, the formula =MATCH(44,A1:A5,0) will return 4, because 44 is the fourth item in the range.

XMATCH is an improved version of MATCH, recently added to Microsoft 365. Unlike MATCH, it works in any direction and returns exact matches by default, which makes it easier to use than its predecessor.

XMATCH is most useful when used as an argument in another function where you need to return the position of a specific item in your data list as one of the arguments of the other function. XMATCH is often used with the INDEX function.

Syntax

```
=XMATCH(lookup_value, lookup_array, [match_mode],
        [search_mode])
```

Argument	Description
lookup_value	Required. This is the value that you want to match in your list. This argument can be a number, cell reference, text, or logical value.
lookup_array	Required. This is the list or range of cells to be searched.
[match_mode]	Optional. This argument enables you to specify a match mode from four options: **0 (or omitted)** - Exact match. If no match is found an error will be returned (#N/A). This is the default if you omit this argument.

-1 - Exact match or the next smallest item, if an exact match is not found.

1 - Exact match or the next largest item, if an exact match is not found.

2 - Performs a wildcard match where you use *, ?, and ~.

[search_mode]   Optional. This argument enables you to specify the search mode to use:

1 (or omitted) - Search first to last. This is the default if this argument is omitted.

-1 - Perform the search in reverse order - last to first.

2 - Perform a binary search (for data sorted in ascending order). If lookup_array is not sorted in ascending order, invalid results will be returned.

-2 - Perform a binary search (for data sorted in descending order). If lookup_array is not sorted in descending order, invalid results will be returned.

XMATCH Examples

In the example below, we use XMATCH to find the relative position of products on the list based on different search criteria. The formulas also use different optional arguments to determine the behaviour of the function.

D2		✕ ✓ fx	=XMATCH(C2,$A$2:$A$11)		
	A	B	C	D	E	F
1	Product		Product	Position	Formula Text
2	Chai		Walnuts	7	=XMATCH(C2,$A$2:$A$11)
3	Syrup		Wal?	7	=XMATCH(C3,$A$2:$A$11,1)
4	Cajun Seasoning		*Oil	4	=XMATCH(C4,$A$2:$A$11,2)
5	Olive Oil		*Sauce	6	=XMATCH(C5,$A$2:$A$11,2)
6	Dried Pears		*Sauce	11	=XMATCH(C6,$A$2:$A$12,2,-1)
7	Curry Sauce				
8	Walnuts				
9	Fruit Cocktail				
10	Chocolate Biscuits Mix				
11	Marmalade				
12	Tomato Sauce				

Formula explanation:

=XMATCH(C2,$A$2:$A$12)

This is a straightforward search for "Walnuts" (cell C2) and the formula returns its relative position of 7 on the list. The optional arguments have been omitted here, so the function uses its default search behaviour.

=XMATCH(C3,$A$2:$A$12,1)

In this example, the *match_mode* argument has been set to 1. This tells XMATCH to find the position of the first item that is an exact match or the next largest value that starts with "Wal".

=XMATCH(C4,$A$2:$A$12,2)

In this example, the *match_mode* argument has been set to 2. This specifies that we are performing a wildcard search, thus, the wildcard characters (*, ? and ~) are treated as special characters.

=XMATCH(C6,$A$2:$A$12,2,-1)

In this example, the *match_mode* argument has been set to **2** for a wildcard search and the *search_mode* argument is set to **-1**, telling XMATCH to start the search from the last item.

You can see that the same search term, "*Sauce" in cells C5 and C6, returned different relative positions (6 and 11). This is because the formula in D5 is searching from the top, as a result, it finds "Curry Sauce" first. Conversely, the formula in D6 is starting the search from the bottom so it finds "Tomato Sauce" first.

INDEX Function - Array Form

The INDEX function in Excel enables you to return a single value or an array of values from a given range. We touch on the INDEX function here as we need to use it with XMATCH to perform simultaneous vertical and horizontal lookups.

There are two forms of the INDEX function:
1. Array form
2. Reference form

For our purposes here, we will be focusing on the array form of the function. INDEX can return a single value, an entire row, or an entire column from a given range.

Syntax

```
=INDEX(array, [row_num], [column_num])
```

Arguments

Argument	Description
array	Required. The *array* argument is a range of cells or an array constant. If the range contains only one row or column, the corresponding row_num or col_num is optional.
row_num	Optional, but if row_num is omitted, then column_num is required. This argument specifies the row in the *array* argument from which to return a value.
column_num	Optional, but if column_num is omitted, then row_num is required. This argument specifies the column in the *array* argument from which to return a value.

Remarks:

- If the *array* argument has more than one row and more than one column, and only Row_num or Column_num is used, INDEX returns an array of the entire row (or column) in the *array* argument.

- INDEX returns a single value (at the intersection of Row_num and Column_num) if both arguments are used.

- INDEX returns an array of values, that is, the entire column or row if you set Row_num or Column_num to 0 (zero).

- To return several values, simply enter the formula in the first cell and press **Enter**. Excel will spill the values to other cells.

INDEX Example

In the following example, we return the sales for "Penny" in Q4 with the following formula:

=INDEX(C6:F17,B3,C3)

C6:F17 is the array, B3 is a reference to the row number, and 4 is a reference to the column number.

D3			f_x	=INDEX(C6:F17,B3,C3)		
	A	B	C	D	E	F
1						
2		Sales Rep	Quarter	Sales		
3			1	4	$22,596	
4						
5		Sales Rep	Q1	Q2	Q3	Q4
6		Penny	$17,526	$23,972	$61,066	$22,596
7		Leslie	$49,405	$36,646	$21,899	$62,629
8		Sally	$78,658	$16,529	$14,976	$68,184
9		Shaun	$80,176	$84,918	$66,561	$65,326
10		Julie	$86,988	$29,692	$30,197	$80,960
11		Velma	$94,514	$13,333	$78,000	$59,718
12		Ian	$23,183	$21,547	$40,408	$57,767
13		Cassandra	$70,597	$19,615	$54,664	$68,175
14		Mark	$16,832	$91,907	$19,062	$23,167
15		Kathy	$45,446	$14,638	$52,312	$92,069
16		Renee	$34,583	$78,213	$21,295	$26,964
17		Judith	$18,689	$91,081	$66,795	$96,860
18						

Using the relative column and row numbers in C6:F17, we can return the sales figure for a sales rep for a given quarter, which is at the intersection of the column number and row number. It would be even better if we can use the name of the Sales Rep and quarter label to return the sales figure. We can do this by combining INDEX with XMATCH.

Using INDEX/XMATCH/XMATCH For Simultaneous Vertical and Horizontal Lookups

On its own, the relative position of an item on a list is not that useful, thus, XMATCH is more useful when used in conjunction with another function like INDEX. MATCH (the predecessor of XMATCH) is often used with INDEX to find and return a value from a specified position on a list. XMATCH provides a simpler and more robust way of performing the same task.

The difference between this method and a simple XLOOKUP is that you are using two given values to look up and return a value.

In the example below, we want to identify the sales amount for a Sales Rep for a given quarter. The combination of INDEX/XMATCH/XMATCH enables us to perform a simultaneous vertical and horizontal lookup.

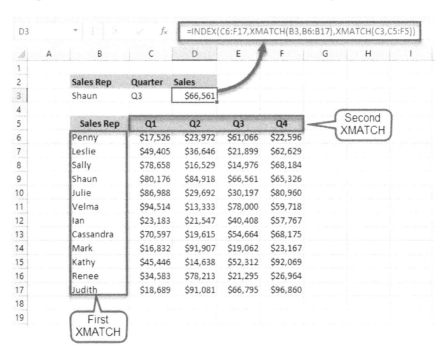

Formula explanation:

=INDEX(C6:F17,XMATCH(B3,B6:B17),XMATCH(C3,C5:F5))

The INDEX function has three arguments. The first argument is the range C6:F17. The first XMATCH function represents *row_num* while the second XMATCH function represents the *column_num* argument.

The first XMATCH function returns **4**, which is the relative position of "Shaun" in range B6:B17, while the second XMATCH function returns **3**, which is the relative position of "Q3" in range C5:F5.

You can use the **Evaluate Formula** command (on the **Formulas** tab) to step through the formula and see the results at each stage of evaluation until it gets to the final arguments used to execute the INDEX function. In the image below, you can see that the *row_num* and *column_num* arguments evaluate to 4 and 3.

=INDEX(C6:F17,4,3)

Evaluate Formula	? ✕
Reference: **Sheet3!$D$3**	Evaluation: = INDEX($C$6:$F$17,4,3)

To show the result of the underlined expression, click Evaluate. The most recent result appears italicized.

| Evaluate | Step In | Step Out | Close |

5. FILTER FUNCTION

The FILTER function is one of the new dynamic array functions in Excel that enables you to filter a range of data based on the criteria you specify. If you are working directly on the source data, you can easily filter it with the **Sort & Filter > Filter** command on the Ribbon. The FILTER function comes in handy for scenarios where you are working on a different range or sheet from the source data.

So, how can FILTER be used as a lookup function? XLOOKUP can be used to return multiple columns from a range, but if you want to return all the columns of a filtered subset of a data list, FILTER is easier to use.

FILTER will return several values which will spill. This means that when you type in the formula and press ENTER, Excel will dynamically create the right-sized range for the return values.

Note: The FILTER function is currently only available to Microsoft 365 users. If you are a Microsoft 365 subscriber and you cannot find this function, your Microsoft 365 installation may be on a semi-annual update plan, in which case you will get the update starting July 2020.

Syntax:

```
=FILTER(array,include,[if_empty])
```

Arguments

Argument	Description
array	Required. The array is the range you want to filter. This can be a row of values, a column of values, or several rows and columns of values.
include	Required. This is a Boolean array (or an expression that includes the criteria range and criteria that evaluates to a Boolean array) whose height or width is the same as the array argument.
	For example, the expression, A2:A10="Apples", will evaluate to TRUE or FALSE for each item in A2:A10. This will determine which values are returned from the range specified in the *array* argument.
[if_empty]	Optional. You can specify a string value to return if the filter returns nothing. For example, "No data".

Remarks:

- FILTER will return a #CALC! error if the return value is empty, as Excel does not currently support empty arrays. To avoid this error, if there is a possibility that your formula will return no records, use the *if_empty* argument to specify a value to return in place of the error.

- FILTER will return an error (#N/A, #VALUE, etc.) if any value in the criteria range is an error or cannot be converted to a Boolean value with the expression in the *include* argument.

- Excel currently has limited support for dynamic arrays between workbooks. Therefore, dynamic arrays that spill to multiple cells will only work when both workbooks are open. If you close a referenced workbook, any linked dynamic array formulas will return a #REF! error when refreshed.

Sample Data for Examples

The sample data we will be using for the examples in this chapter will be on a separate sheet named **SalesData** in the workbook. As the sample data is in a different worksheet, any reference to cells or ranges in the data will be prefixed by the worksheet name, for example, SalesData!A4:E51.

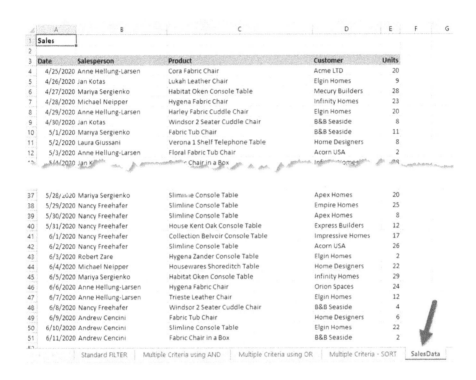

	A	B	C	D	E	F	G
1	Sales						
2							
3	Date	Salesperson	Product	Customer	Units		
4	4/25/2020	Anne Hellung-Larsen	Cora Fabric Chair	Acme LTD	20		
5	4/26/2020	Jan Kotas	Lukah Leather Chair	Elgin Homes	9		
6	4/27/2020	Mariya Sergienko	Habitat Oken Console Table	Mecury Builders	28		
7	4/28/2020	Michael Neipper	Hygena Fabric Chair	Infinity Homes	23		
8	4/29/2020	Anne Hellung-Larsen	Harley Fabric Cuddle Chair	Elgin Homes	20		
9	4/30/2020	Jan Kotas	Windsor 2 Seater Cuddle Chair	B&B Seaside	8		
10	5/1/2020	Mariya Sergienko	Fabric Tub Chair	B&B Seaside	11		
11	5/2/2020	Laura Giussani	Verona 1 Shelf Telephone Table	Home Designers	8		
12	5/3/2020	Anne Hellung-Larsen	Floral Fabric Tub Chair	Acorn USA	2		
13	5/4/2020	Jan K	Chair in a Box	Inf Homes			
37	5/28/2020	Mariya Sergienko	Slimline Console Table	Apex Homes	20		
38	5/29/2020	Nancy Freehafer	Slimline Console Table	Empire Homes	25		
39	5/30/2020	Nancy Freehafer	Slimline Console Table	Apex Homes	8		
40	5/31/2020	Nancy Freehafer	House Kent Oak Console Table	Express Builders	12		
41	6/1/2020	Nancy Freehafer	Collection Belvoir Console Table	Impressive Homes	17		
42	6/2/2020	Nancy Freehafer	Slimline Console Table	Acorn USA	26		
43	6/3/2020	Robert Zare	Hygena Zander Console Table	Elgin Homes	2		
44	6/4/2020	Michael Neipper	Housewares Shoreditch Table	Home Designers	22		
45	6/5/2020	Mariya Sergienko	Habitat Oken Console Table	Infinity Homes	29		
46	6/6/2020	Anne Hellung-Larsen	Hygena Fabric Chair	Orion Spaces	24		
47	6/7/2020	Anne Hellung-Larsen	Trieste Leather Chair	Elgin Homes	12		
48	6/8/2020	Nancy Freehafer	Windsor 2 Seater Cuddle Chair	B&B Seaside	4		
49	6/9/2020	Andrew Cencini	Fabric Tub Chair	Home Designers	6		
50	6/10/2020	Andrew Cencini	Slimline Console Table	Elgin Homes	22		
51	6/11/2020	Andrew Cencini	Fabric Chair in a Box	B&B Seaside	2		

Standard FILTER | Multiple Criteria using AND | Multiple Criteria using OR | Multiple Criteria - SORT | SalesData

Note: The above sample data will be used for all examples in this chapter. You can download this file from the web link included in this book.

How to Create a Drop-down List

The examples in this chapter will employ drop-down lists for selecting the criteria to be used for filtering our data, thus, this section briefly goes over how to create a drop-down list in an Excel cell. If you already know how to create a drop-down list, then you can skip this section and go directly to the FILTER examples below.

Note: Creating a drop-down list is not essential as you can simply type in the value in the cell. However, being able to select the value directly from the source data saves time and reduces errors.

Follow the steps below to create a drop-down list:

1. Select the cell in which you want to create the drop-down list. For example, cell B3 in a blank worksheet.

2. On the **Data** tab, in the **Data Tools** group, click on the **Data Validation** command button and select **Data Validation** from the drop-down menu.

    This will open the **Data Validation** dialog box.

3. On the **Settings** tab, in the **Allow** box, select **List** from the drop-down list.

4. Next, click in the **Source** box, then select the data range you want to display in your list. For the example, in this chapter, you would click the SalesData sheet tab (at the bottom of the workbook) and then select range C4:C51 on the worksheet with your mouse. Excel will automatically enter the selected range in the Source box.

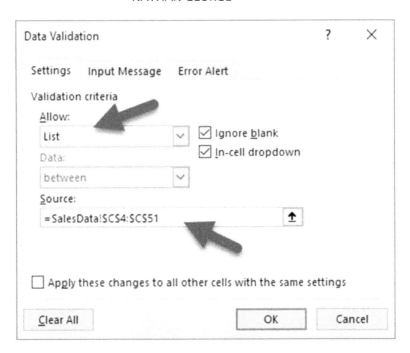

5. The **Ignore blank** and **In-cell** checkboxes should be checked by default. If not, then check both of them.

    We do not need the Input Message and Error Alert tabs for this exercise.

6. Click on **OK** to finish creating the drop-down list.

When done, the drop-down list will display a list of values from the selected source when you click the drop-down arrow.

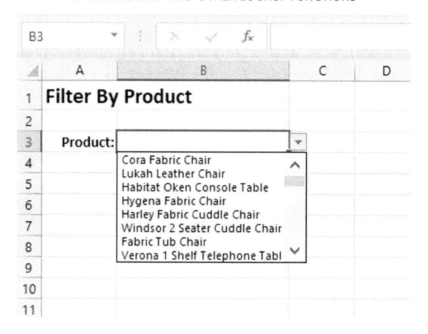

Simple FILTER Example

In this example, we want to return a subset of records from our data list in the SalesData sheet by filtering it with a product name.

The filtered data is to be displayed on a different worksheet from the SalesData sheet. On the new worksheet, cell B3 has a drop-down list bound to SalesData!C4:C51. This enables us to select a product name for the *Product* column of our data list.

The column headings of the data list have also been copied (from SalesData) and pasted in cells A5:E5.

The formula is entered in cell A6. When you press **Enter**, the returned values (if there are any) will spill into the other cells in the spill range.

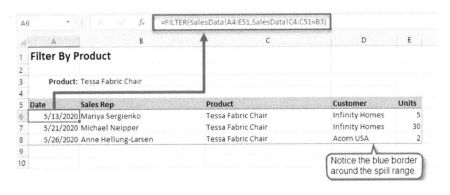

Formula explanation:

=FILTER(SalesData!A4:E51,SalesData!C4:C51=B3)

The *array* argument has a reference to the full list we are seeking to filter and return. This is range A4:E51 on the SalesData worksheet, which is a separate sheet from the one with our formula.

Our *include* argument is an expression that will generate a Boolean array from the criteria range. The criteria range is SalesData!C4:C51. When we compare it to the value in B3 using the equal sign (a comparison operator), the expression will evaluate to TRUE or FALSE for each value in the criteria range.

```
SalesData!C4:C51=B3
```

You can step through the formula using the **Evaluate Formula** dialog box to see the result of the expression SalesData!C4:C51=D3. It evaluates to a Boolean array.

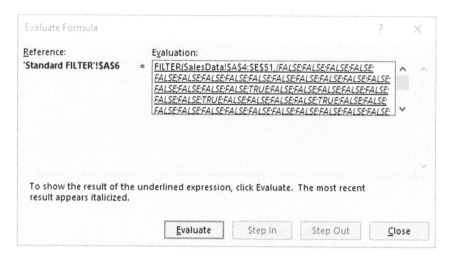

The values that evaluate to TRUE are the ones that determine which records are returned in the filtered data.

Note: Chapter 7 covers how to step through an Excel formula using the Evaluate Formula dialog box.

Multiple Criteria Filter using AND

In this example, let's say we want to return all entries in our data list with the same Product **AND** Sales Rep. This will be a multiple criteria filter. To achieve this with the FILTER function, we use the multiplication operator (*) to include additional Boolean arrays to the *include* argument.

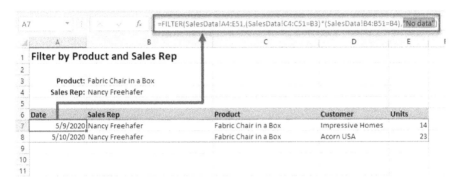

Formula explanation:

=FILTER(SalesData!A4:E51,(SalesData!C4:C51=B3)*(SalesData!B4:B51=B4) ,"No data")

The value in the *include* argument has two expressions separated by the multiplication operator (*), indicating we only want to return records for which BOTH expressions evaluate to TRUE.

(SalesData!C4:C51=B3)*(SalesData!B4:B51=B4)

As there is a possibility of having no records when we filter the data using the combination of a product and a sales rep, "No data" has been entered in the *if_empty* argument. This value will be returned in cases where the return value is empty.

Multiple Criteria Filter using OR

In this example, we want to return all entries in our data list (A4:E51) with a given Product **OR** a given Sales Rep. To achieve this, we use the addition operator (+) to include additional Boolean arrays to the *include* argument.

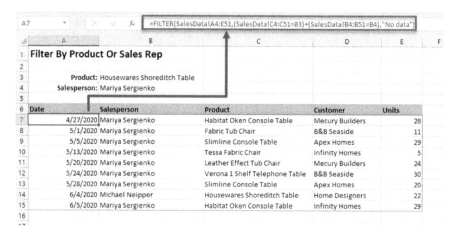

Formula explanation:

=FILTER(SalesData!A4:E51,(SalesData!C4:C51=B3)+(SalesData!B4:B51=B4),"No data")

The value in the *include* argument has two expressions separated by the addition operator (+).

(SalesData!C4:C51=B3)+(SalesData!B4:B51=B4)

This indicates we want to return all records where at least one of the expressions evaluates to TRUE.

Sorting Filtered Data

In this example, we want to return all entries in our data list (A4:E51) with a specified Product **OR** a specified Sales Rep. Additionally, we want to sort the data in descending order using the **Units** column so that the records with the highest units show first.

A7		fx	=SORT(FILTER(SalesData!A4:E51,(SalesData!C4:C51=B3)+(SalesData!B4:B51=B4),"No data"),5,-1)				
	A	B	C	D	E	F	G
1	**Filter By Product Or Sales Rep - Sorted**						
2							
3		Product: Housewares Shoreditch Table					
4		Salesperson: Mariya Sergienko					
5							
6	Date	Salesperson	Product	Customer	Units		
7	5/24/2020	Mariya Sergienko	Verona 1 Shelf Telephone Table	B&B Seaside	30		
8	5/5/2020	Mariya Sergienko	Slimline Console Table	Apex Homes	29		
9	6/5/2020	Mariya Sergienko	Habitat Oken Console Table	Infinity Homes	29		
10	4/27/2020	Mariya Sergienko	Habitat Oken Console Table	Mecury Builders	28		
11	5/20/2020	Mariya Sergienko	Leather Effect Tub Chair	Mecury Builders	24		
12	6/4/2020	Michael Neipper	Housewares Shoreditch Table	Home Designers	22		
13	5/28/2020	Mariya Sergienko	Slimline Console Table	Apex Homes	20		
14	5/1/2020	Mariya Sergienko	Fabric Tub Chair	B&B Seaside	11		
15	5/13/2020	Mariya Sergienko	Tessa Fabric Chair	Infinity Homes	5		
16							
17							

Formula explanation:

=SORT(FILTER(SalesData!A4:E51,(SalesData!C4:C51=B3)+(SalesData!B4:B51=B4),"No data"),5,-1)

This formula is like the one in the previous example, but the FILTER function has been nested in a SORT function.

Briefly, the **SORT function** is a dynamic array function that takes in an array and returns a sorted list, based on the sort_index and sort_order you have specified.

Syntax:

```
=SORT(array,[sort_index],[sort_order],[by_col])
```

In our formula, we have specified a sort_index of **5**, indicating we want to use the fifth column in our data list for the sort.

For the sort_order, you have two options: 1 is ascending order and -1 descending order. Our formula has a sort_order of **-1** which specifies we are sorting the data in descending order.

6. ERROR HANDLING FUNCTIONS

When working with Excel formulas you may encounter the #N/A error, which happens when the formula cannot find the lookup value. In this chapter, we will look at the two main functions you can use to handle expected formula errors.

IFERROR Function

IFERROR is used to trap errors in Excel formulas and return a meaningful message, just like how errors are trapped and handled in computer code. IFERROR will return the value you specify if the formula evaluates to an error. Otherwise, it returns the result of the formula. IFERROR can trap the following error types: #VALUE!, #N/A, #DIV/0!, #REF!, #NAME?, #NUM!, or #NULL!.

Syntax:

```
=IFERROR(value, value_if_error)
```

Arguments

Argument	Description
value	Required. This is the expression that is checked for an error. This can be a value, cell reference, or a formula. When using IFERROR with VLOOKUP, the VLOOKUP formula will be this argument.
value_if_error	Required. This is the value you will enter for the formula to return when Excel encounters any of the errors listed above.

IFNA Function

The IFNA function is specifically for handling the #N/A error. It will return the value you specify if your formula returns the #N/A error, otherwise, it returns the result of the formula.

Syntax:

= IFNA(value, value_if_na)

Arguments

Argument	Description
value	Required. This is the expression that is checked for an error. This can be a value, cell reference, or a formula. When using IFNA with VLOOKUP, the VLOOKUP formula will be this argument.
value_if_na	Required. This is the value you will enter for the formula to return when it encounters an #N/A error.

The difference between **IFERROR** and **IFNA**

Use IFERROR when you want to trap and handle all kinds of errors. As mentioned above, the IFERROR function traps a variety of errors, even those caused by mistakes in the formula. It would not matter to IFERROR what caused the error, it would replace the error with your specified value.

Use IFNA when you want to trap and handle only #N/A errors. In certain scenarios, you may only want to trap #N/A errors as they are more likely generated when formulas cannot find the lookup value. You usually would want to display other errors as they may reveal bugs in your formula that need to be fixed.

Note: The IFNA function is not required for use with XLOOKUP as it already has a built-in #N/A error handling feature.

7. HOW TO STEP THROUGH A FORMULA

Have you ever had a formula that was not producing the expected result, but you can't pinpoint the source of the error? In this chapter, we will cover how to 'step through' a formula. Sometimes a formula can be complex with several nested levels. In a complex formula with several intermediate evaluations and logical tests, it may be difficult to keep track of the sequence of operations and the intermediate results from each nested function. Thus, formulas that fail to produce the desired result may include logical errors that are difficult to spot at the surface.

The good news is that Excel has a tool named **Evaluate Formula** that allows you to step through a formula so you can see how the different levels of the formula are being evaluated, what the logical tests are doing, and the results returned at each level. This will enable you to identify and resolve any logical errors in the syntax.

Example

In this example, we will use the Evaluate Formula command to step through the following formula to see what the internal functions are doing:

=SUM(XLOOKUP(F3,A2:A30,D2:D30):XLOOKUP(G3,A2:A30,D2:D30))

The formula is using two nested XLOOKUP functions to select a range that we want to sum.

The way a multi-level formula works is that the nested functions are evaluated first, then the returned results are used as arguments for the outer function.

With the Evaluate Formula dialog box, we want to see the breakdown of the results of the individual evaluations before the formula returns the final result.

The data being evaluated is shown in the image below.

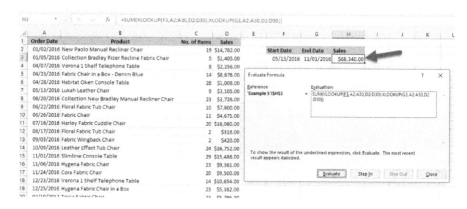

To evaluate a formula, follow the steps below:

1. Select the cell that you want to evaluate. In our example, it is cell **H3**. Note that only one cell can be evaluated at a time.

2. On the **Formulas** tab, in the **Formula Auditing** group, click on the **Evaluate Formula** button. This will open the Evaluate Formula dialog box.

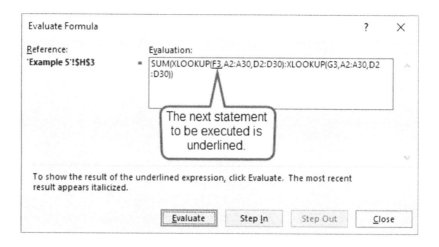

First, we see the formula in the **Evaluation** box with the next expression to be executed underlined.

3. Click the **Evaluate** button to examine the underlined part of the formula. The result of the evaluation will be shown in italics, and the next statement to be executed will be underlined.

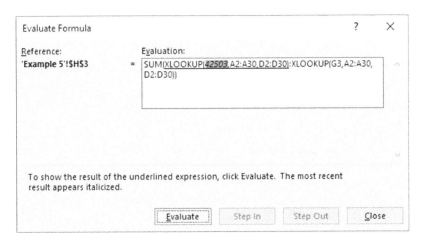

If the underlined part of the formula is a reference to another formula, you can click the **Step In** button to display that formula in the Evaluation box. When done, click **Step Out** to go back to the original formula.

The **Step In** button will not be enabled for a cell reference the second time it appears in the formula, or if the formula refers to a cell in a different workbook.

4. When you click on the Evaluate button again, you will see the result returned by the nested formula. In this case, it returns a cell reference ($D$7).

Note: A neat feature of XLOOKUP is that it can return a cell reference or range when nested. Thus, we can dynamically build a range based on lookup values.

5. When you click on **Evaluate** again, the next expression to be evaluated will be underlined, and so on, until the final result is reached. At this point, the Evaluation button will be changed to **Restart**, which enables you to go through the process again.

6. When done, click **Close** to dismiss the **Evaluate Formula** dialog box.

Note: Some functions are recalculated each time the worksheet changes, thus the Evaluate Formula dialog box could give results that are different from what appears in the cell. The following functions may not work well with Evaluate

Formula: RAND, OFFSET, CELL, INDIRECT, NOW, TODAY, RANDBETWEEN, INFO, and SUMIF (in some scenarios).

APPENDIX: SHORTCUT KEYS FOR WORKING WITH DATA, FUNCTIONS, AND THE FORMULA BAR

The table below covers some of the most useful Excel for Windows shortcut keys when working with functions, formulas, and the formula bar.

Keystroke	Action
F2	Moves the insertion point to the end of the contents of the active cell.
Ctrl+Shift+U	Expands or reduces the size of the formula bar.
Esc	Cancels an entry in the formula bar or a cell.
Enter	Confirms an entry in the formula bar and moves to the cell below.
Ctrl+End	Moves the cursor to the end of the contents in the formula bar.
Ctrl+Shift+End	Selects everything in the formula bar from the current position of the cursor to the end.
F9	Calculates all worksheets in all open workbooks.

Shift+F9	Calculates the active worksheet.
Ctrl+Alt+F9	Calculates all worksheets in all open workbooks, even if they have not changed since the last calculation.
Ctrl+Alt+Shift+F9	Checks all dependent formulas and then calculates all cells in all open workbooks.
Ctrl+A	Opens the Function Arguments dialog box, when the insertion point is to the right of a function name in a formula bar.
Ctrl+Shift+A	Inserts the argument names and parentheses for a function when the insertion point is to the right of a function name in the formula bar.
Ctrl+E	Executes the Flash Fill command to fill-down the current column, if Excel recognizes patterns in the values in adjacent columns.
F4	Changes the selected cell reference or range in the formula bar to absolute references. Further presses will cycle through all combinations of absolute and relative references for the selected cell reference or range.
Shift+F3	Opens the Insert Function dialog box.
Ctrl+Shift+Quotation mark (")	Copies the value from the cell directly above the active cell into the active cell or formula bar.
Alt+F1	Automatically inserts an embedded chart of the data in the selected range.
F11	Automatically inserts a chart of the data in the selected range in a different worksheet.
Alt+M, M, D	Opens the New Name dialog box for creating a named range.
F3	Opens the Paste Name dialog box if a range name has been defined in the workbook.

Alt+F8	Opens the Macro dialog box where you can run, edit, or delete a macro.
Alt+F11	Opens the Visual Basic for Applications editor.

GLOSSARY

Absolute reference

This is a cell reference that does not change when you copy a formula containing the reference to another cell. For example, $A$3 means the row and column have been set to absolute.

Active cell

The cell that is currently selected and open for editing.

Alignment

The way a cell's contents are arranged within that cell. This could be left, centred or right.

Argument

The input values an Excel function requires to perform a calculation.

AutoComplete

This is an Excel feature that completes data entry for a range of cells based on values in other cells in the same column or row.

Backstage view

This is the screen you see when you click the File tab on the ribbon. It has a series of menu options to do with managing your workbook and configuring global settings in Excel.

Boolean array

A Boolean array is an array of TRUE/FALSE Boolean values or (0 and 1). In Excel, you can create such an array by applying logical tests to the values in a column or row.

Cell reference

The letter and number combination that represents the intersection of a column and row. For example, B10 means column B, row 10.

Conditional formula

A conditional formula calculates a value from one of two expressions based on whether a third expression evaluates to true or false.

Dynamic array formula

Dynamic array formulas are a set of new formulas in Excel that enable you to return multiple results to a range of cells from one formula. This is called the spill range.

Excel table

This is a cell range that has been defined as a table in Excel. Excel adds certain attributes to the range to make it easier to manipulate the data as a table.

Fill handle

This is a small square on the lower-right of the cell pointer. You can drag this handle to AutoFill values for other cells.

Fill series

This is the Excel feature that allows you to create a series of values based on a starting value and any rules or intervals included.

Formula

An expression used to calculate a value.

Formula bar

This is the area just above the worksheet grid that displays the value of the active cell. This is where you enter a formula in Excel.

Function

A function is a pre-defined formula in Excel that just requires input values (arguments) to calculate and return a value.

Named range

A group of cells in your worksheet given one name that can then be used as a reference.

Relative reference

Excel cell references are relative references by default. This means, when copied across multiple cells, they change based on the relative position of columns and rows.

Ribbon

This is the top part of the Excel screen that contains the tabs and commands.

Sort

A sort means to reorder the data in a worksheet in ascending or descending order by one or more columns.

Spill Range

This is the range of cells that contains the results returned from an array formula. This range can be multiple rows and/or columns.

Workbook

This is the Excel document itself and it can contain one or more worksheets.

Worksheet

A worksheet is like a page in an Excel workbook.

AFTERWORD

Thank you for buying and reading this book. I hope it will serve as a great Excel resource for you in the months and years to come. If you have any comments or suggestions for how this book can be improved even further, please feel free to contact me at nathangeorgeauthor@gmail.com.

For more help with Excel functions, you can visit Microsoft's help site for Formulas and Functions.

Note: The official link is far too long and convoluted, so I've made it accessible with a simple click on my website.

Website link:
https://www.excelbytes.com/microsoft-excel-help/

More on Excel

For more Excel content, visit my website:

https://www.excelbytes.com/

You will find free tips and techniques on various Excel topics, including new developments in Excel.

INDEX

ABOUT THE AUTHOR

Nathan George is a computer science graduate with several years' experience in the IT services industry in different roles, including Excel programming and providing end-user support to Excel power users. One of his main interests is using computers to automate tasks and increase productivity. As an author, he has written several technical and non-technical books.

OTHER BOOKS BY AUTHOR

Excel 2019 Basics

A Quick and Easy Guide to Boosting Your Productivity with Excel

Excel 2019 Basics covers all the essentials you need to quickly get up to speed in creating spreadsheets solutions for your data.

If you are new to Excel and the thought of spreadsheets makes your head spin, then this is the right book for you. This book will hold your hand through a step-by-step process in becoming skilled with Excel.

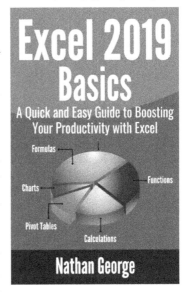

If you already have some Excel skills and you want to skill-up on more advanced topics like functions, Excel tables, charts, and pivot tables then this book is also for you.

Excel 2019 Basics goes beyond introductory topics and covers topics like functions, Excel tables, and analysing your data with charts.

The aim of this book is to guide you from beginner to being skilled with Excel within a few short hours.

Excel 2019 Advanced Topics

Leverage More Powerful Tools to Enhance Your Productivity

Whether you have basic Excel skills or you're a power user, *Excel 2019 Advanced Topics* is full of methods and tips that will enable you to take advantage of more powerful tools in Excel to boost your productivity.

Excel 2019 Advanced Topics covers a selection of intermediate to advanced topics relevant to productivity tasks, you're more likely to perform at home or work.

This book does not only show you how to use specific features but also in what context those features need to be used.

Excel 2019 Advanced Topics explains how to automate Excel with macros, use What-If Analysis tools to create alternate data scenarios and projections, analyze data with pivot tables and pivot charts, debug formulas, solve complex data scenarios with advanced functions, use data tools to consolidate data, remove duplicate values from lists, create financial formulas to carry out financial calculations, and much more.

Excel 2019 Functions

70 Top Excel Functions Made Easy

Do you want to delve more into Excel functions and leverage their full power in your formulas?

Excel functions are predefined formulas that make it easier and faster to create solutions for your data.

Excel 2019 Functions provides comprehensive coverage of 70 of the most useful and relevant Excel functions in various categories including logical, reference, statistical, financial, math, and text functions.

Learn how to use many advanced functions introduced in Excel 2016/2019 like the IFS function which can replace convoluted nested IF functions.

This book also comes with lots of Excel examples which you can download as Excel files, so you can copy and use the formulas in your own worksheets.

Excel 2019 Functions will be a great resource for you whether you're a beginner or experienced with Excel.

Excel 2019 Macros and VBA

An Introduction to Excel Programming

Do you often perform repetitive tasks in Excel that can be time consuming?

You can automate pretty much any task in Excel with a macro.

If you want to automate Excel, *Excel 2019 Macros and VBA* will be a great resource for you.

We start from the very basics of Excel automation, so you do not need any prior experience of Excel programming.

You will learn how to automate Excel using recorded macros as well as Visual Basic for Applications (VBA) code. You will learn all the programming essentials to start creating your own VBA code from scratch.

Excel 2019 Macros and VBA will enable you to create solutions that will save you time and effort, create consistency in your work, and help to minimize errors in your Excel projects.